A Kid's Guide to Puerto Rico

A lookout tower (and historic landmark) at Castillo San Felipe del Morro, San Juan, Puerto Rico (see page 10).

Curious Kids Press • Palm Springs, CA
www.curiouskidspress.com

On September 20, 2017, Hurricane Maria, a devastating Category 4 hurricane, made a direct hit on Puerto Rico. It caused massive damage on the island and killed more than 45 people.

According to the governor of Puerto Rico, Hurricane Maria was "probably the single biggest hurricane catastrophe in the history of the U.S."

Despite the tireless effort of FEMA (the Federal Emergency Management Agency) and other disaster relief workers, many of the residents of Puerto Rico still did not have electricity for their homes or gasoline for their vehicles weeks after the storm.

The magnitude of this disaster was enormous. Yet, the governor of the island promised that the island would rebuild, and that once again the island would become the beautiful paradise that so many people know and love.

To aid in the relief effort, Curious Kids Press is donating ten percent of the net proceeds from the sale of this book to the American Red Cross, specifically earmarked to help the American citizens affected by Hurricane Maria.

Publisher: Curious Kids Press, Palm Springs, CA 92264.
Designed by: Michael Owens
Editor: Sterling Moss
Copy Editor: Janice Ross

Table of Contents

ON THE COVER: The Puerto Rican Parrot, one of the rarest birds in the world and only found in Puerto Rico. See page 17.

BIRTH OF THE NEW WORLD *is the name of a huge statue of Christopher Columbus which stands on the Atlantic coastline of Puerto Rico. The statue is 360 ft. (110 m) tall, 45 ft. (13.7 m) taller than the Statue of Liberty.*

Welcome to

Puerto Rico

Official Name: Commonwealth of Puerto Rico

Capital City: San Juan

Total Area (Size): 3,515 sq. miles (9,104 sq. km) About twice as big as the U.S. state of Rhode Island

Population: 3,351,827 (about the same as the city of Madrid, Spain)

Official Language: Spanish and English

IN 1493, ONE YEAR AFTER HIS FAMOUS VOYAGE TO THE NEW WORLD, Christopher Columbus made a second trip to the Americas. It was then he first stepped foot on an amazing island in the Caribbean. He immediately claimed that island for the Crown of Castile (later, Spain) and named it San Juan Bautista (or Saint John the Baptist).

Four hundred years later, in 1898, this island became a territory of the United States, and in 1917, all people of the island who were born after 1898 became United States citizens.

Today, that island is known as Puerto Rico, meaning "rich port." It is an island with a rich and colorful history and lots of fun things to do. Let's explore this island paradise.

PUERTO RICO HAS MORE AMERICAN CITIZENS then 21 of the U.S. states put together. Yet, those citizens cannot vote in the election of a president of the United States.

Here are some other facts about the island and its people.....

- Voters in Puerto Rico can vote in primary elections to nominate a candidate in the Republican, Democratic, or other political party.
- Puerto Ricans can be drafted (when a national military draft is in effect).
- Puerto Ricans pay Social Security and Medicare tax, but do not pay federal income tax.
- Puerto Ricans can travel within the U.S. without a passport.

Where in the World is Puerto Rico?

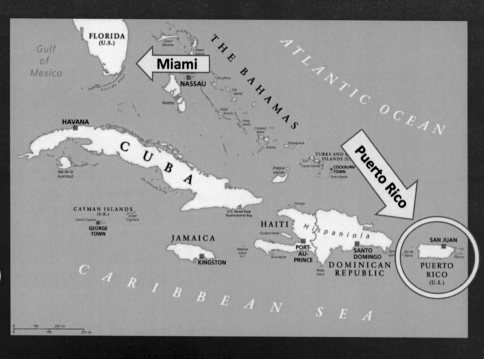

PUERTO RICO IS AN ISLAND between the Caribbean Sea and the North Atlantic Ocean. It is approximately 1,000 miles (1609 km) from Miami, Florida.

Puerto Rico is an **archipelago** among the Greater Antilles. The Greater Antilles is a grouping of islands in the Caribbean Sea, including Cuba, Hispaniola (containing Haiti and the Dominican Republic), Puerto Rico, Jamaica, and the Cayman Islands. Puerto Rico is the smallest of those islands.

The Commonwealth of Puerto Rico has more than 143 islands, but only three are inhabited – Puerto Rico, Vieques, which is 8 miles (13 km) east of Puerto Rico, and Culebra, which is about 17 miles (27 km) east of Puerto Rico.

Did You Know?

Puerto Rico is only a hundred miles (161 km) long by 35 (56 km) miles wide.

A Brief History of Puerto Rico

1493: Christopher Columbus discovers the island during his second voyage to the Americas. He claims it for the Crown of Castile (later, Spain).

1873: Slavery is **abolished.** (Today, Puerto Rico celebrates Emancipation Day on March 22 each year.)

1898: Puerto Rico is **ceded** to the United States as a result of a war between Spain and the United States (known as the Spanish-American War).

1917: Puerto Ricans are granted U.S. citizenship.

1952: A constitution is enacted that gives Puerto Rico the right to govern itself.

1960s: Thousands of immigrants arrive in Puerto Rico from Cuba, as they escape Fidel Castro's Communist state.

2017: A **referendum** showed that 97 percent of the citizens who voted were in favor of statehood. (However, only about 23 percent of the registered voters voted.)

2017: A Category 4 hurricane devastates the island in September.

Cool Facts About
Puerto Rico

Maracas (gourds filled with pebbles or dried beans and mounted on handles) are musical instruments that were created and first used by the Tainos of Puerto Rico. The unique sound they make is common in Puerto Rican music.

Puerto Rico is home to a teeny-tiny tree frog (one-inch long) called the coquí. See page 16.

The only tropical rainforest in the U.S. National Forest System is in Puerto Rico (see page 12).

Even though Puerto Rico is a territory of the United States, it competes individually in the Olympics.

Puerto Rico has 273 miles (439 km) of beachfront.

Luis Muñoz Marín is regarded as the "Father of Modern Puerto Rico." He was the first democratically elected Governor. Puerto Rico's International Airport is named for him.

The Mona Ground Iguana is found only on Mona Island, Puerto Rico, an uninhabited island except for overnight campers and government personnel.

Puerto Rico is known for its beautiful beaches. But there is one beach that has black sand. It is known as Playa Negra (or, of course) "Black Beach."

The Taino people lived on the island of Puerto Rico for hundreds of years before Christopher Columbus arrived. They called the island *Boriquén Tierra del alto señor* ("Land of the Noble Lord").

One traditional style of music in Puerto Rico is Bomba. It is a mixture of Spanish, African, and native Taíno music.

Originally, Puerto Rico was the name given to the area now known as Old San Juan. It was only later that the whole island became known as Puerto Rico.

FUN THINGS FOR KIDS TO DO IN PUERTO RICO:

EXPLORE EL MORRO

NEARLY 500 YEARS AGO, in 1539, King Charles V of Spain decided to build a **citadel** (or fort) to defend the port of San Juan, Puerto Rico. It was called Castillo San Felipe del Morro.

Originally, it was a small fort with only a few men standing guard and four canons. Then, in 1765, the King of Spain decided to enlarge El Morro to the huge structure that exists today. It took about 150 years to complete.

Over the years, the fort was attacked many times. But it was never defeated by an attack from the sea, and fell only once (briefly) in an attack from land.

Today, the fort is known simply as El Morro. With its many dungeons and passageways, and tunnels and turrets, El Morro is a fun place for kids to explore.

EL Morro *El Morro has six levels that rise 145 feet (44 m) above sea level.*

1. Main Access
2. Green Field Leading to Entrance
3. Dry Moat
4. Main Plaza
5. Main Artillery Ramp
6. Main Battery
7. Lower Patio
8. The 1939 Tower
9. Water Battery
10. Harbor Entrance'

A large green field in front of the fort is a popular place for picnics or to fly kites – a favorite activity for kids in Puerto Rico.

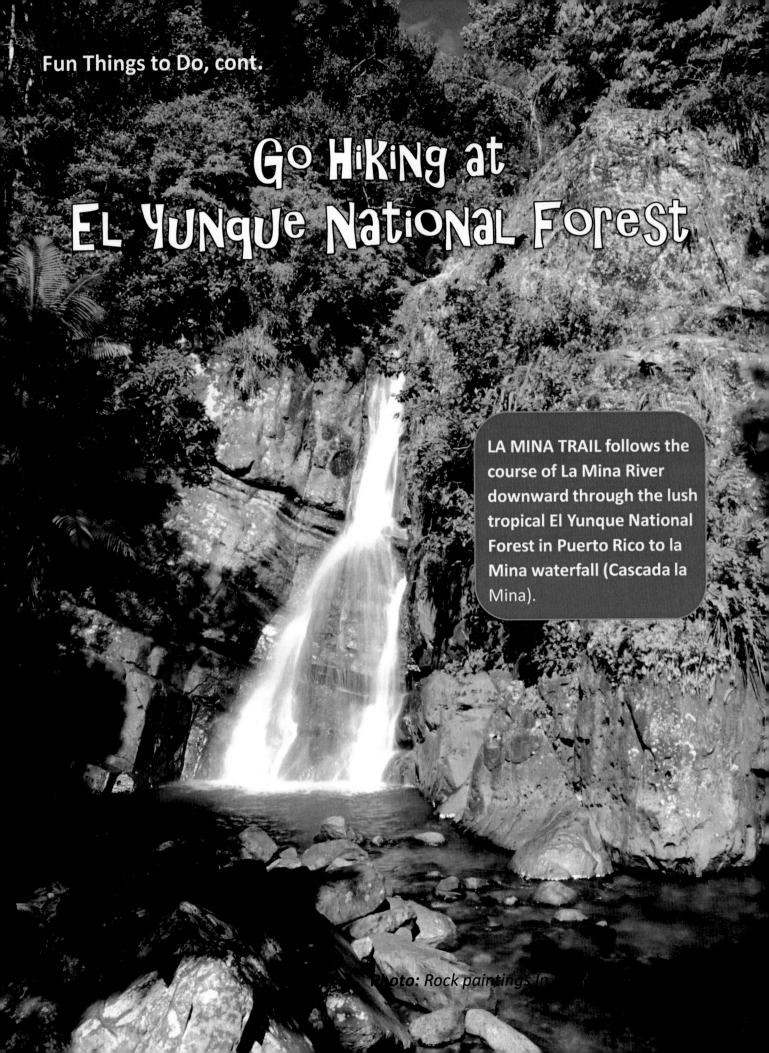

Go Hiking at El Yunque National Forest

LA MINA TRAIL follows the course of La Mina River downward through the lush tropical El Yunque National Forest in Puerto Rico to la Mina waterfall (Cascada la Mina).

Photo: Rock paintings In

and the Caribbean Sea, all at the same time? Then, hike up Mt. Britton Trail. There, you'll find a lookout tower built in the 1930s. From the observation deck of the tower, on a clear day, you can see forever – or so it seems.

Mount Britton is one of the highest points in El Yunque National Forest, the only tropical rain forest in the United States National Forest System.

The forest is filled with some amazing wildlife. There are at least 50 different species of birds, 11 species of bat, 8 species of lizards, and 13 species of coqui, a tree frog. There are even five or six species of non-poisonous snakes, though they are rarely seen in the forest.

Mt. Britton Lookout Tower

There are other trails that are great for hiking at El Yunque, including El Yunque-La Mina, which leads to the stunning La Mina waterfall (see opposite page). There is also El Toro Peak that will take you to the highest point of the forest at 3,532 feet (1076.6 m) above sea level.

Did You Know? The U.S. National Forest System consists of 155 National Forests. If put all together, the 155 forests would fill the entire state of Texas.

Try SPELUNKING* IN Camuy

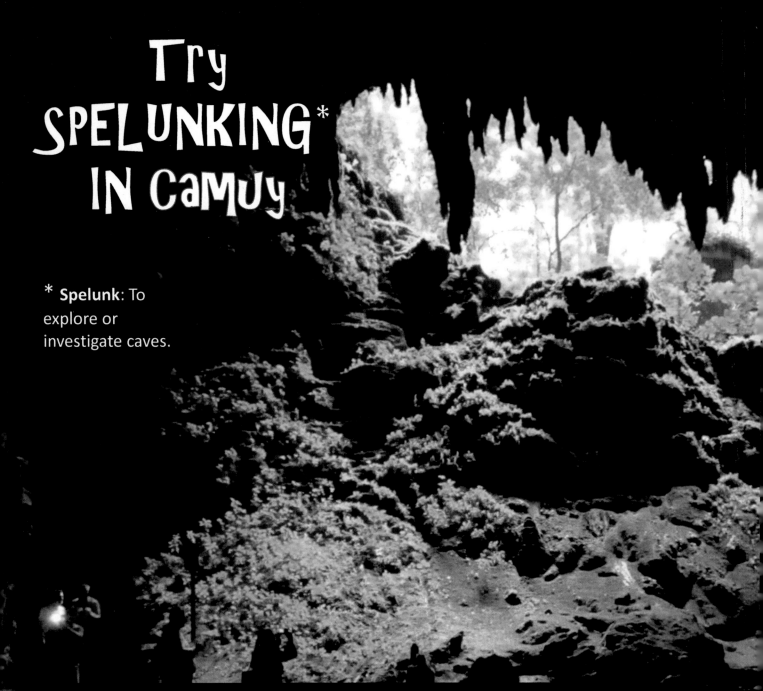

* Spelunk: To explore or investigate caves.

WOULD YOU LIKE TO GO SPELUNKING?

A fun place to do that in Puerto Rico is at Camuy River Cave Park (Parque nacional de las Cavernas del Rio Camuy).

The limestone caves and underground waterways were carved out by the third largest underground river in the world, the Rio Camuy (Camuy River) many years ago.

Today, more than 220 caves have been discovered, though expert spelunkers believe there are as many as 800 more in the entire cave system. Yet, only two caves and three **sinkholes** are open to the public.

Inside the cave, you will discover **stalactites**, **stalagmites**, unique formations – and thousands of bats. (Bats love caves.) And you will, too.

Cave Words to Know

Cave: An underground cavity that is formed naturally by the dissolving action of acidic groundwater.

Cavern: A large cavity found within a cave.

Chamber: The largest type of cavity in a cave.

Sinkholes: Bowl-shaped depressions that are created by the collapse of an underground cave.

Spelunker: A person who enjoys exploring caves

Speleologist: A person who studies the geology, formations, and environments of caves and cave systems.

Stalactite: A cave formation that develops from the cave ceiling and hangs downward.

Stalagmite: A cave formation that develops from the cave floor and protrudes upward.

Troglodyte: A human cave dweller.

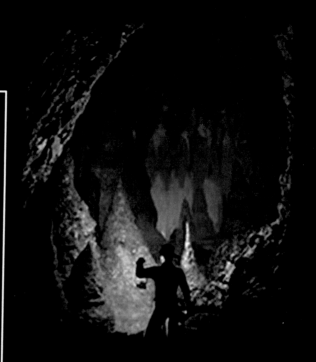

The cave system was only recently discovered, but hundreds of years ago the caves were explored by the Taino Indians, Puerto Rico's first inhabitants (see page 20).

The largest cave open to the public measures 170 ft. (51.8 m) at its tallest point.

One of the sinkholes measures 650 ft. (195 m) wide. The Camuy River can be seen 400 ft. (120 m) below it.

Before You Go: There are no bathrooms inside the cavern. So be sure to "go" before you go.

WiLDLiFe oF PueRto RiCo

RAIN FORESTS AROUND THE WORLD are known for their **biodiversity**. They are home to more than half of the world's animals – from tiny insects to large **mammals**.

El Yunque, the rain forest in Puerto Rico, is no different. Hundreds of different kinds of animals live in the forest.

But one thing you won't find in El Yunque is any "big" wildlife, such jaguars or monkeys.

Still, there are plenty of birds, reptiles, and small **mammals** in the forest, some of which are only found on this special island. Here are some of them.

El Coquí. Imagine holding a frog on the tip of your finger. You can do that with El Coqui, a tiny frog known for the sound it makes. (The length of its body is about 1 inch (34 mm), although its legs are at least as long a its body, sometimes longer. El coquí is the national symbol of Puerto Rico and is known for the loud sound it makes at night, which sounds like co-kee. It's endemic (only found) in Puerto Rico.

The Antillean Manatee. It's not a rain forest animal. But it is an amazing mammal found in the waters of Puerto Rico.

They're sometimes called "sea cows." Take one look and you can probably guess why. It's a fish, but it doesn't look like any fish you've ever seen. They look like a fat floating cow...or at least a dolphin.

This marine mammal is 8 to 15 feet long and weighs, on average, 400-600 kilograms.

Because they are mammals, they must come up for air about once every 15 or 20 minutes.

Their nostrils are like little valves that can remain tightly closed when they dive under water.

THE PUERTO RICAN PARROT (aka the Puerto Rican Amazon) is one of the ten rarest birds in the world. And it's only found in Puerto Rico.

When Christopher Columbus first arrived on the island, there were hundreds of thousands of this small, beautiful bird.

But, over the years, the forests where the parrot lives were cut down to make room for farms and villages.

Today, sadly, there are only about 60 to 80 left in the rainforest of Puerto Rico. They are on the endangered list, meaning there is a chance they will become **extinct** in a short period of time.

The Puerto Rican Parrot measures about 11.8 inches (30 cm) long.

Lizards of Puerto Rico

There are at least 50 different kinds of lizards on the island of Puerto Rico, including geckos and green iguanas, which can reach 6 feet (1.8 m) in length and weigh up to 15 pounds (6.8 kilograms). Imagine!

But the most common lizards in Puerto Rico are anoles. There are at least 10 different species or kinds. They range from 3 inches (76 mm) to 7 inches (17.8 cm) in length. Anoles can change their color from brown to bright emerald green.

The Puerto Rican crested anole is found throughout Puerto Rico .

The Puerto Rican spindalis is the national bird of Puerto Rico. It is found only in Puerto Rico.

Experience Bioluminescence in Mosquito Bay

HAVE YOU EVER WATCHED a group of fireflies (or lightening bugs) at night? It's fun to try to catch them in a jar as they zip around, flashing their light on and off.

The **emission** of light from the firefly (or other living organisms) has a rather long name. It's called *bioluminescence*.

Fireflies aren't the only bioluminescent **organisms** on Earth. There is another kind that lives in the sea. It's call a dinoflagellate. (You can call it dino, for short.)

One of the best places to see bioluminescence from dinos is at Mosquito Bay on the island of Vieques, which is part of the Commonwealth of Puerto Rico.

The dinos in the bay there produce a brilliant blue-green color in the water whenever they are disturbed, such as when you paddle around in a kayak, or drag your hand through the water.

You'll be amazed at this magical experience. It may even be more fun than catching fireflies on a summer's night.

The Story of the Taíno Indians

IN 1493, DURING HIS SECOND VOYAGE TO THE NEW WORLD, Christopher Columbus stepped foot on a large tropical island in the Caribbean. There, he met a group of very friendly people who brought Columbus and his men food and gifts.

"Taino, taino," the people said to Columbus, which, in their language, means "We are good people." Columbus, however, thought they were telling him the name of their tribe. And today, these people are known as the Taíno.

The Taíno had come to the islands of the Caribbean from South America more than two thousand years before Columbus met them. They settled in what is today Jamaica, Cuba, and Hispaniola. They also settled on the island of Puerto Rico, where Columbus and the Taíno first met.

The Taíno were a peaceful, friendly, and generous people. They had their own religion and their own culture. They worshipped and gave thanks to a divine being, called Yocahu.

They grew corn and sweet potatoes, among other crops. They lived in small villages, called *yucayeques*. They built large round houses called *bohio*. They slept on cotton hamacas (like today's hammocks).

A modern example of an old Taíno village.

In the center of a typical village was a central plaza. It was used for various social activities, such as games, festivals, and religious ceremonies.

For fun, the Taino often played a game called *batey*. It was played with a ball made of rubber from the juice of trees. Columbus was fascinated by the rubber ball. Rubber was unknown in Europe at the time.

For a while, the Taíno and the Spanish colonists got along. But soon life for the Taíno changed. The Spaniards took Taíno men from their villages and forced them to work in gold mines and on colonial plantations. As a result, the Taíno were not able to plant their own crops to feed their own people.

In addition, the Spaniards brought strange diseases, such as measles, to the island. The Taíno had never experienced such diseases. They had no **natural immunity**. In 1519, a smallpox epidemic killed most of the Taíno population.

When Columbus first arrived, approximately three million Taíno lived on the islands of the Caribbean. Less than 30 years later, there are fewer than a thousand.

English Words That Come from the Taíno Language

Taino	English
Hamaca	Hammock
Barbacoa	Barbecue
Juracán	Hurricane
Kanoa	Canoe
Tabaco	Tobacco
Batata	Potato

What's to Eat?

How about "mofongo." It's found everywhere on the island.

A "mofongo" starts with mashed plantains (sort of like mashed bananas). It's fried with a lot of other ingredients. It's found everywhere on the island. BTW, plantains are sometimes called the pasta of the Caribbean.

Schooling and Education: What's the Difference in Puerto Rico?

In Puerto Rico, the words schooling (*instrucción)* and education (*educación)* have very different meanings. Schooling is what you learn in school from books and your teacher. Education has to do with learning to be respectful, polite, and courteous.

Games Kids Play

Have you ever played Blind Man's Bluff? In Puerto Rico, kids play a similar game. But they have a different name for it. It's called "The Blind Little Hen." To play, everyone gets in a big circle. One person is chosen as "The Blind Little Hen" and is blindfolded and turned around three times. The hen then must identify someone in the circle simply by touching his or her face. The person identified then becomes "The Blind Little Hen."

Try it. It's fun!

Holidays in Puerto Rico

Puerto Ricans celebrate all of the same holidays that are celebrated in the United States. But they also have some holidays that are not national holidays in the United States. One is Puerto Rico Constitution Day (Día de la Constitución del Estado Libre Asociado), which is celebrated on July 25 each year. It marks the day the Puerto Rican constitution was signed into law.

Glossary

Archipelago (*noun*): A group of islands or body of water in which they are located.

Biodiversity (*noun*): The existence of many different kinds of plants and animals in an environment.

Citadel (*noun*): A fortress built on a high place in or near a city.

Emission *(noun):* The act of producing or sending out something.

Mammal (*noun*): Any animals with a backbone that feed their babies with milk from their mothers.

Natural immunity: Protection (usually from a disease) that is either present at birth or acquired (usually through vaccination).

Organism (*noun*): Any single living being, such as an animal, plant, fungus, etc.

Referendum (*noun*): The practice of voting on an issue or question.

Hope you enjoyed reading this book about my country.

Please leave a review at Amazon.com

Adios!

For Beginning Readers

Available as E-book or Print Edition!

Curious Kids Press

The Elephant Picture Book

With original photography of the elephants at Boon Lott's Elephant Sanctuary in Thailand.

Ages 4-7

By Jack L. Roberts
With Photography
by Michael Owens

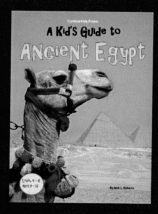

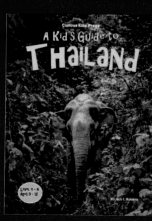

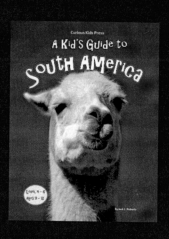

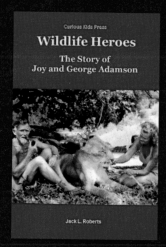

A Kid's Guide to
Puerto Rico
For Parents and Teachers

About This Book

A Kid's Guide to . . . is an engaging, easy-to-read book series that provides an exciting adventure into fascinating countries and cultures around the world for young readers. Each book focuses on one country, continent, or U.S. territory, and includes colorful photographs, informational charts and graphs, and quirky and bizarre "Did You Know" facts, all designed to bring the country and its people to life. Designed primarily for recreational, high-interest reading, the informational text series is also a great resource for students to use to research geography topics or writing assignments.

About the Reading Level

A Kid's Guide to . . . is an informational text series designed for kids in grades 4 to 6, ages 9 to 12. For some young readers, the series will provide new reading challenges based on the vocabulary and sentence structure. For other readers, the series will review and reinforce reading skills already achieved. While for still other readers, the book will match their current skill level, regardless of age or grade level.

About the Author

Jack L. Roberts began his career in educational publishing at Children's Television Workshop (now Sesame Workshop), where he was Senior Editor of The Sesame Street/Electric Company Reading Kits. Later, at Scholastic Inc., he was the founding editor of a high-interest/low-reading level magazine for middle school students. Roberts is the author of more than a dozen biographies and other non-fiction titles for young readers, published by Scholastic Inc., the Lerner Publishing Group, Teacher Created Materials, Benchmark Education, and others.. More recently, he was the co-founder of WordTeasers, an educational series of card decks designed to help kids of all ages improve their vocabulary through "conversation, not memorization."